DETROIT
(MAIDEN ENERGY)

Detroit Street Princess Poems & Lyrics

CAROLYN STRIHO

AQUARIUS PRESS/AUXMEDIA
Detroit, Michigan

Detroit (Maiden Energy)

© 2019 by Carolyn Striho

All rights reserved. No part of this publication may be reproduced, stored in a retrieval system, or transmitted in any form, or by any means, electronic, mechanical, recording, photocopying or otherwise without the prior written permission of the publisher.

Front cover photo: Scott Dailey
Back cover photo: Patricia Izzo

ISBN 978-1-7330898-3-8

Aquarius Press
www.AquariusPress.net
PO Box 23096
Detroit, MI 48223

In Association with AUXmedia
www.AUXmedia.studio
440 Burroughs, Ste. 117
Detroit, MI 48202

LIST OF LYRICS of PUBLISHED SONGS
ALBUM/CD/EP/VINYL/CASSETTE

"Midnight Stars" —*Afterthought* (2016)
"One More Time" —*The Sound & The Fury* (1984)
"Maiden Energy" —*Live Traxx* (1984)
"Apple" —*Word Attack* (2013)
"Island" —*Dreams Can Be Your Friend* (1995)
"Necklace" —*Secrets and Space* (2000)
"Cornered Room" —*Afterthought* (2016)
"Visions" —*The Sound and the Fury* (1984)
"Terrible Twos" *Thanks for Nothing* (1992); *Dreams Can Be Your Friend* (1995)
"Put Me In A Trance" —*The Sound and the Fury* (1984)
"Shadow" —*Detroit Energy Asylum* (1986) 12" EP Vinyl
"Circles" —*Honesty* (2009)
"Tiara" —*Is This Me?* (2008) and *Word Attack* (2013)
"Honesty" —*Honesty* (2009)
"Sing It To Me" —*Honesty* (2009)
"January Baby " —*Honesty* (2009)
"Ocean" —*Is This Me?* (2008)
"Out In The Streets" —*The Sound and the Fury* (1984)
"Blast off Black Magic" —*(Compilation Rough Cut)* (1983)
"Free" —*Afterthought* (2016)
"Stay There" —*Theatre of the Night* (1988)
"Giftwrapped in Cool" —*Detroit Energy Asylum* (1986) 12" EP
"Enchante" —*Is This Me* (2008); *Word Attack* (2013)

Printed in the United States of America

Contents

I. Poems about Growing Up

Back in the Garden	9
Running on Ice	11
Midnight Stars	12
Detroit Street Princess	14
LIFE 1977	15
City Music Lights	16
Little Horses	17
One More Time	18
Maiden Energy	19
Sometimes I Drink	22
hurt day	23
Member of the Club	24
Fainting in a Church	25

II. Poems about Love and War

Apple	29
Begin Again	31
Do You Think It's Fair?	32
Hate Calls	33
November Rain	34

III. Songs of Love

Island	39
Necklace	40
Cornered Room	41
love pour	42
Redemption	43
Visions	46
Terrible Twos	47
Enchante	48
Put Me in a Trance	49
Sensing the Sun	50
Shadow	51
Shiver	52
Circles	53
Tiara	55
Honesty	57
Sing it to Me	59
January Baby	61
Ocean	62
Out in the Streets	63
Blast off Black Magic	65
Free	66
Gracious Spoke	67

Magician of Darkness	68
Not My Design	69
Stay There	70
Transcendance Captured from a Distance	71
Something Special	72
Cold Summer June	73
Italy	76
One More Road (into the night)	77
Romantic River of Weird Times	78
King of the Road	79
Sun Blues	80
April is the Cruelest Month	81
Giftwrapped in Cool	82
About the Author	85

Hi. I've been wanting to do this for a while, and being a songwriter most of my life, I wanted to share some of my own poetry and lyrics. Some have been published through music, but many poems have never been published or performed. So, it's an exciting endeavor!

I grew up in Detroit, and as a little girl, took piano lessons, sang in choirs, and loved my little diaries and poems. Our house was filled with music. When I began to make up songs, I wanted to learn from the musicians and music I heard. So I tried guitar, too. I had a bit of a voice, so singing, writing, and playing in a band seemed natural. I guess my bands and I had that youthful rebel feel and we went through heady times in a big music time back then and now.

These poems, ideas and dream sequences are part of thoughts and random ideas and writing. Some are lyrics of songs I've recorded and published, which came out on vinyl, cassettes and CDs. Others are poems or small stories of street life, angst, strength, nature and hard times of Detroit, but the contrast with street beauty and power of the City, and Michigan.

And I hope you can read between the lines a bit and find some humor and love with a defiant strength and energy in overcoming hard situations. Detroit is a very hard town, unlike anywhere else, but a beautiful place and part gritty city and gorgeous country. Finding passion and humor in the middle of everything is a secret of life!

At the risk of the book being too long, I included what I could for now as I have many more lyrics that came out with songs on albums I didn't include in this book here. I'm working on another book, and wanted some of my poetry in this first book. There are hundreds of posters, fliers and photos of a big, expansive musical life I wanted to include, but for the sake of time and space, we're mainly focusing on the words right now.

I've always been a bit of a loner and introvert who identifies with the underdog. My mom would say, "Be your original self, who cares what people think?" Thus, the title is tongue-in-cheek, yet timely, for so many girls and maybe anyone who needs confidence, courage and hope.

Life can be quite daunting, but there's a ray of hope always. And hopefully, the writing makes you think a bit?

That's all.

Love,
Carolyn
2019

I. Poems about Growing Up

Back in the Garden

Back in the garden
rhubarb and berries
this is in the city
Detroit beauty
  nobody knows
all of the trees
all of the forest
is my magic
believed.

the kids came over
they played in the attic
we hid and found
  four leaf clovers
folded the hope and put in the Bible of autumn leaves
like a revival

I fell down the stairs and rolled my head
to the hard wood floor
until I saw
red

back in those days
life was a haze of sun ripened tomatoes
and skinned knees
I always hit the hardest
I always cried the hardest
8 years old at my aunt's funeral in an old Plymouth car

how do you get here?
how do you start?
when you're world is so thick
and your mind is so smart?

where did you go?
and how do you get there?
when your northern spirit
keeps pushing along
sand dune summers

ice cold winters
music head and voices yelling loud
languages we spoke to understand
when your brain is moving faster than your body
ever can

how do you get there?
when northern spirit
keeps pushing along

behind the garages, hop over fences,
ivy on brick
the beautiful city
  running so hard
exciting streets with my bike hitting
concrete summer heat

Back in the garden
rhubarb and berries
this is the city
of Detroit beauty
  nobody knows of all of the trees
all of the forest is my magic believed

Running on Ice

Like running on ice,
fell down, so frozen
I needed direction
or some kind of discovery
I heard electric sounds and excited hounds barking
all night long

I asked her name, but she began once again
to hallucinate some coffee grounds of disorder and chaos

Militant armies and black colored grass
and a fort stood near me so I ran unaware
 of fear or distaste

(dirty hair/wash the pain off my face)
Clothes a façade for my loss of an angle
Drinking ice cold beer in the dead of winter
crawling to jungles of drifting mirages

If only I had something warm,

But no one was near, no one could hear any battle cries
of a survivor after space's race on the hemisphere
with teeth, and eyes, arms here and there

So I was running on ice, hoping for some comfort on the last day.

Before I fell asleep, I prayed and saw the angels breaking the stars
in silent violence, and it seems they looked hard at me
They stopped to stare and dropped pillows of sunshine on my
torn body

I could stop running for awhile, and I always remembered to stay
away from the black and white spiders' webs.

Midnight Stars

chaotic fantasy escape meditate
street hurts painful deals in the night on a dream
crashing cars let me down to a bleeding book of burning
branches ghosts warm the night when we're all alone
in a panic
of love and rain

midnight stars erase
memories
I need to remember
birdland skies and night train rope
blackbird train they running dope (hope)
all the way, I need to remember
what's always in my heart

I overdo it to bring up energy
like Beethoven pouring buckets of water
over his head
I do it
so I'm not dead
doesn't everybody wake up feeling sick?

why is it that happens
just
the
next
time
I can count too many handfuls and waves of pure angst snowing
in the deserted mind
then next filled with buckets of pain
depression? someone says that
silly word that describes nothing

the basement is too cold
and I think a shadow went right by
my world hurts
and sometimes it is only the answer
to feel that dark black hurling in your mind
showing up to dark corridors where others smile, happy

you try to explain, nobody is listening
so you take to writing
nobody then can complain
or if you complain, they take it wrong
they don't understand
it's all one big surface of show
surface of blowing your face up
and it's not a bit real

I watch all the "should have" I meant to,
I would have and realize they couldn't have
they don't have it
they don't have sincerity or background
living in a city,
living with defending
they have never had to defend a damn thing

Living in two when bright lights hurt
bright sun blurts out a ribbon of resentment
I feel like I've got to run and get something to drink
only not water
to shut down the sun that's only good in the summer

sun in the winter's too icy and hurts my forehead
it's ok on the back, my back's bent over from years of moving
so fast I can't see
now the world is vacantly humming too quickly
but like glass, it is broken more swiftly than ever
sharp ends praise the Lord, pass the sword
and wrap my arms around my self
only, one arm is broken
one ear is roaring
from yelling and loud sounds
and my heart is hardly speaking
to me
anger and sadness that spread
across my eyes
and twilight always mocking me
don't remember the drive
just I'm here and I'm alive

Detroit (Street Princess)

Stands in the litter
but gorgeous energy lights the sky
dirt in the mouth
but gold in the heart
future and past stand side by side
all your dreams are mine
We stay, watching cement block the river
watching death on the doorstep
smell barbecue
smell barf
smell a sense of cosmopolitan highlights
fight the opponent
stay awake
stand proud
hand in holster
don't shoot
just smother the urgent violence
land clean
land a mess, a place for total contradiction
video me in, radio me in,
don't fade out now
you're starting to smell better
ghetto flower
streetlight princess
racing in the beauty and delicate
crossroads, we face the enemy
smiling

LIFE 1977

Sounds kept him waiting
Or maybe he had to wait in the line
He stayed to praise something
there was his friends
in their cars
going faster
chasing in a triangle
mysterious black triangle
appearing on the wall
He muttered, "some sorcery" and
called to his pills and girls
go on outside
crawl, fast asleep
down the highways
as you try to find
something to do
Wants some MEANING
in the streets
Tired of revulsion of
routine
reads Bibles, Stones, lyrics,
tries to paint a canyon
Don't let me do it
don't tie a noose too tight
give me
a little longer
needs some money
beg, borrow, steal
Handclap, handtrap
He's only one person
but wants more out of it.

City Music Lights

Got to get going
Detroit rock and roll
under my fingers
with delicate soul

you can't believe it
it hasn't been told
harder and harder
dance passion the goal

this isn't explained in words
just by action
expression extension
of my own ascension

to take all inside
and let it come out
from the streets, from the city
never a doubt

from the Lodge to 7 mile
and near Van Dyke
Belle Isle music
we played every night
Rosedale Park over to Cass Avenue

Back near The Southfield
the clubs with a view
to Plymouth Road and under
by the tracks southwest
Mexican Village to the backstage mess
we went in those old cars
we walked on the road
down to Masonic Temple
where we were living large

Marshall amps downtown
in places all the rage now
Midtown was Cass Corridor
home of the free and the brave

loving the vision of the wild road
loving the incision of the guitar load
we traveled everywhere in the streets so bold
wasn't called the after party 'cause it was just cold

we're out in the streets
we're out on the stage
things haven't changed

we're ambassadors of music made
in the motor city it was never a deal
because writing and performing is
what makes us real

One More Time

I can't tell you what I mean
Everyday I get these screams
My concentration's underground
Mystery without a sound

One more time, you call me over
No, don't you get in my memory
Like crazy words flowing, now you got yours
Qui va va, qui va va instead

Feel the urban escape
I can't see your shadowed eyes
Shock and sock your face through me
I can't tell you what I see

One more time, you call me over
No, no, don't you get in my memory
Like crazy words flowing, now you got yours
Qui va va, va va instead

Just give me one more time

Maiden Energy

Well, we slept all right
But we woke up one night
alert in a circle
with a scraped guitar surface
on my medallion.
And then I heard this ringing
it sounded like a holiday
but it's better than a holiday

Go on kick anyway, go out in the world,
this is a brave hard noise, Maiden Energy

She thinks she's a tiger at night, they give her a birthday flight
Well, man, come on let's go, got to take her on the road

I played guitar onstage, felt like a target,
with one devil in the hall
so something's going to happen

Go on kick anyway, go out in the world
this is a brave hard noise, Maiden Energy

Little Horses

All the little horses be with me again
Seems the stream's awakening
like an old friend
All the little horses connecting within
Remember your heartbeat sense you begin

Then we walked in the ride
When we toughened our pride
We were holding our leather, so strong and then
We were just so alive
We were starting our stride…
The door was opening, stronger, stronger

You spoke…my eyes were blackened again
Like a long-lost friend
Black and smeared with endless sadness when you walked in

All the little horses just like my dreams
Riding the hilltops, deep river dreams
The country closer when you touch my face
Your body warm love being holding my pace

My eyes are so bright it's a long summer's night,
The cold's letting in, fire growing within
I didn't know my mind,
I can't say the sign that finally gave me energy
to trust and be kind

And the strong city girl
Was just like a whirl
Trying so hard
And then you came and took me by surprise
Like the words were right
Because the Night
Ready for lovers, you hold me tight

All the little horses
Come back home again
This isn't the end

Come a little closer, put your lips on mine
Come a little closer, it's finally time
All the little horses be with me again

Sometimes I Drink

Sometimes I think
if I hadn't had that drink
to taste what she had was the end

Sometimes she reeks
when she smokes and she pinks
pain as it chips on the mirror

Sometimes the rink
that she skates in her mink
in the snow I remember
the cold

Sometimes he sinks
into miserable stink
of the smell of the dim moldy hole

Sometimes she drinks
from a well of not-think
to stray from her hurtful link
soul

Sometimes I sink
into misery links
the painful cold snow
Detroit is April time flow

And sometimes I think
if I hadn't had that drink
to taste what she had
was the end

hurt day

I kind of think
that you're a jerk
she told him, singing and laughing
but he was drunk and slammed the door
right on her leg, she ran out of the car
it hurt, it sped fast
I guess it doesn't matter if you're a so-called angel
when you get hit by the devil
it's the same thing when you don't want anything
to hurt you
it always does hurt you
then the day is gone and it's another one

member of the club

love is what it is
is it anything at all
liars but lovers, shit for brains
I was asking someone about it
what it meant when you broke up
with him
what it meant when I broke up with him
it didn't matter, he didn't care
but what if he did? I can't know but I dug my nails into my skin
and decided pulling a hair out might help with something,
anything. a teenager, you know how it is
dramatic, but what if you were slammed to the ground
does that memory go away with time and maybe it doesn't
then does it matter, I'm going to work anyway

Fainting in a Church

when I was a little kid, but not that small, just starting to feel a bit of angst a riding on the wall
somebody came running up the stairs, yelling my sister had fainted
the voice sounded unfamiliar like someone I didn't' know
only it was my mom, running from the bathroom, all dressed up
for church, on fire, the wires outside dangling with birds
I wasn't sure what to do and didn't want to get blamed for my sister fainting
then she fainted in church on the altar. I thought for sure she was dead
and I would get blamed
just because I was big sister
and I would be shamed
because I was scared
and the priest carried her in his arms
and I silently
ran
down the
church basement stairs
to make sure it wasn't on fire (I was still alive)

1979

Feel brain strain
Don't want to go all the way there
don't stop, heat overload
but go onward to a new challenge

He was debating her, a ruby jewel in her opal eyes,
a sleek black cat in the pouring rain, outside
 the theatres and nightclubs.

She nodded, he knew, tore off the magic cloak of darkness
Looking for the light,
the object of the search
white line skin, needle felt nothing,
forget the numbness, just to feel
Her face racing
The bells rang, so he stopped
for a moment
at an abstract street of overwhelming beauty

Like, the Land of Oz, kaleidoscope
of sound and vision

Staccato prints ripped his mind
Knew lust, love, artistic pleasure in her mind's attic

Swim and wade together, the rain pours
flowers of dust, and clouds of
Hot ingénue, she gave him her sweat
She did and he did
Overheat, music of the streets,
Sounds elevate them together

II. Poems about Angst & War

Apple

The apple is not like picture
it is the real juice dripping
   the bit of your teeth
marking me
marking me
red and courageous

I walk proud wearing scars
 as I stumble into it again
 hurt and sick, with pain so thick
   could never remedy

only without you I'm lost
and now it's underneath
   underwater, like a strong comet
or crisp in autumn
 room in my heart

 so sore
so lonely, you're like a
little kid

I keep hearing that I can't keep up

rabbits running distant
maybe I'll keep just one
   close to me
as nobody says you can have 2

still life, still life remains
life is the opening of our veins
the waterfall hurtling into my eyes
 when the light bursts so hard

but like bruises on an apple
that's where I'm at
splitting my heart hurts everybody
sick scissors, sick lizards letting
the slow crawl to death's doorstep

mornings are worse
they creep up on the clock
horrific squinting
tossing, hot, ill, have to get up
on the dark side
no brightness in my eyes
   or my mind until afternoon solstice
as I walk wounded and crying
   hiding tears as professional as I can

Sometimes I can't believe
Is This Me?

Begin Again

All the confusion couches the coast
rocks, rain, ruin return again

inside, harder, happens to me, but happens to be
the one quick avenue of alive in the pain

Birds floating, singing loud,
sun shining, seems so rude to leave
Detroit's beginning so fast

hurtling hurdles of hard crunch as shoes hit pavement
near the river again

again and again
the city won't end
just begging to begin again

scatters our blood and only pretends

to not care, when it's very soul depends on our love

through the hate we consider, watching the dove

spread its wings over water and splash as it flies

away from the smokestack, away sunrise…

away from rocks, rain, ruin, return again

again and again
the city won't end
just begging to begin again

Do you think it's fair

It's not really fair
Do you think it's fair
to be stuck in this world
with all of this fear

wear bracelets and crystals
to ward off the bay
of water rushing in
and challenge a day

stems from the hate and the war in the world
just never stops and the news is a whirl of
killings and gunfighters
who spade the earth

stems from a puddle I put underneath
to catch some relief
in awe of what we have while others lose sleep

all of our troubles and some cannot eat

been spinning and running through long weighted grass
green gloves of clover and falling through glass

neighbors may watch or turn quickly away
when the trigger is pointed by policemen today

Color is nothing, yet color it is
skin dark or white, the gun wasn't his

then neighbors can call but they watch eyes so near
as we shake, then eyes get larger with fear

It's not really fair
do you think it's fair

Hate Calls

Really need to know
make a choice
envious interesting
turn to harassment
hotline

we can live wherever we want
burn crosses on everyone's lots
you sick people, you tyrants alone
look at yourself
look at your home

talk all the time how good you are
you know everything
you sit back armchair quarterback
and think you're president

that's a weird analogy
we know the boss is nuts
the man in charge has checked out before
they are not in touch

Serious/law enforcement
late night America
don't talk much to me
white argue black argue
everyone disagree
no response
seem to think and probably so
the details are too gross
incidents too numerous to count
jump up, toleration
you never see a cross on a white lawn

hate calls and hate calls
preaching to you, come home to me
I'll teach you to kill whatever spirit you had
when a kid puts it away
your propaganda rages and you lost it

November Rain

Can't help but crying
remembering pain
but why is it back
in November rain
Michigan Central,
on a Detroit train
why is it back
in November rain

remember the birds
 in wide awake words
nothing can help when you feel so absurd
but you could cry
you could scream
so try to be happy.
Resoundingly free

and one more line and back on the run
drinking from stolen bottles of fun
 splitting sidewalks gritty with rum
the love and the hope has all come undone

 don't want to do this, want to spread laughs
sinking, I'm sinking, she's split up her raft
scared to make choices, so frightened again
she's beautiful but ugly is her only friend,

sun go away, please sun stop, it hurts
please give me some drugs or something, she blurts
it's the something she doesn't know what she has
it's already ok, but she's lost in the jazz
of what might save her, music is key
to live inside pain is a new energy
so she resolves to driving downtown
to pick up the pieces with another round

Can't help but crying
remembering pain
constant remembering

November rain
Michigan Central
starting the train
in the streets of Detroit
she decides to remain

III. Songs of Love

Island

I live by a breath of fate you were into fast mistakes
you always in my heart, surround my blood now I start.

I feel anxious. ready to move.
don't you stand far, I'm searching for you.
Breaking through lights, creating a scene
You now hear yelling. you're locked in a dream

I blast off it feels so good, I land in your arms.
And tonight I knew I would.

on the screen you look larger than life.
I can feel your voice flowing to me.
Blue and purple and fire like ice, so charming and pretty.
I know your pillow so well, your drink is not fresh, you're not sleeping well.
I open the letter in the yellow sand…
The road looks timbered it's like an old man.

I blast off it feels so good, I land in your arms.
And tonight I knew I would.
land in your arms
Island in your arms
I land in your arms..

Necklace

A Pacino act, an Empress piano
A purring panther reminds me of a singer
This is good, this is the way I want it
Out from the city out in the fields

Crystal pane necklace around my throat
Don't keep tugging or it will get broken and
This little necklace around my throat
Stop this tugging or you will be broke and all alone

Confused but laughing, crazy but happy
Flowers growing in the snow
Must be a freak garden growing
Then you tell me it's a winter apricot plant
Will bloom anywhere, anywhere that it grows

Crystal pane necklace around my throat
Don't keep tugging or it will get broken and
this little necklace around my throat
Stop this tugging or you will be broke and all alone

I'm falling, I'm falling down...
I'm falling, I'm falling,
On the ground, rolling, rolling
I'm falling, don't want to be on the ground
underground

A Pacino act, an Empress piano
A purring panther reminds me of a singer
This is good, this is the way I want it
Out from the city out in the fields
Out from the city out in the fields
Out from the city out in the fields with a
Crystal pane necklace around my throat
Don't keep tugging or it will get broken and
This little necklace around my throat
Stop this tugging or you will be broke and all alone'

Cornered Room

When every corner of the room begins to empty out and I can see what you've done

The sun is going down and the rain is falling hard on your face as you withdraw

Pretending is easy, but it's not so pretty, take leave of your feelings, like the ocean all separating

You've got this illusion, you are the everything in my window you're on your own.

A fate for you, afraid of me
What do you think about it when you're on your own?

I cut the paper really fine just like I cut you
Go ahead and get out of your lie,
take another corner of the room.

Sunday is already here and the rain is falling
on your face as you withdraw

The corners of the room so big, the corners of the room just draw you back in

Pretending is easy, but it's not so pretty
Take leave of your feelings like the ocean all separating
You've got this illusion
You are the everything in my window
you're on your own.

And like the sea, you rush to me, what do you think about it when you're on your own? I cut the paper really fine just like I cut you

Go ahead and get out of your lie,
go ahead and get out of your lie

Go ahead and get out of my life,
Take another corner, always in the room.

love pour

Love is like a luxury
love I need and love to thee
hold my heart so close to you
this romantic ingénue

kind of like Rumi
kind of like Khalil Gibran
tells us how love
is the root of the land

gorgeous breathing from your soul
unite with my story untold

lavender daydreams, breeze so soft
caresses your body, so beautiful tough

your skin is so golden
the fields and the lake
hold us together
and love is our fate

fast beauty
thank you, dear Lord
for the love and the faith
that you have poured

over the streams
and the hills nearby
So grateful and happy
to not say goodbye

Redemption

Remembrance
little girl
follow your heart
follow your smarts

I want to concentrate on you
too much to do

just be careful

frozen wastes
the land as the rich see fit
down in the deep bright whole
a human race contemplates suicide

apples and oranges mixing together
we find a simplistic answer
to everyone's problems

stop the clock, lose control
praises, praises as they strike for their wages
just please don't go away now

God and devil stand off in the distance
choose your weapon, choose your sword

They take their pens and rub them on the page
rub them further and forthright
waiting for a message
like waiting for Godot
you know that's one long wait
they left me steaming on the beach out of reach

factories stand motionless
as the sea disguises itself in the belly
of a nuclear whale

where are you going?
loneliness prevails,

emptiness of jails
countries have customs their own
where no people can roam
they want to shoot you on the spot
loot for a popsicle
burning the New York Times in anger

All I want is a sweet song
get lies
hear none, see nothing but hypocritical truths
Where is it coming from?
bursting women to the sea
ice fairies, song canaries
and ladies sewing silk

You read the psalms, you know them well but I guess that doesn't matter

fire of the heart
attack of the street concrete
Is this the rainbow of restraint?
or we do bow to the money god

children play in the mud in the middle
scrub wafers near the priest

just please don't go away now

silence is too loud
try to block out the sound of nothing
redemption of the saviour
fire of our neighbor

the slaves look daily for their daily bread
everything's too tight and we hope for salvation
life manifested in concern and worry

Remembering children
and huge imagination
big crates of singular pain
hurled onto their minds

A ruler from afar
sets his war watch
on the waiting
for the right time
phrases repeated
wish you were here

Don't send them that
give them a wish
candle wax melting
give them hope
in your sleep
energy of a lifetime
as we wonder where time fled

Please don't go away now

Visions

A long night
the way you tore me on my knees

I can't write
easier to spell and read

Visions I get them
when I'm all alone
Whenever I get them
I'm on my own

He thought that
his ancient charm could set him free
that's all right,
he's drinking excess in the bar with me

Visions I get them all of the time
Whenever I get them, my body will rhyme

I felt so chromatic, the feeling intense
Pupils dilating, body immense
See what you're doing by leaving me here
I don't want no reception from all of your fear!

Visions I get them all of the time
Whenever I get them, my body will rhyme

You know how it is when the church bells chime
and you're running real fast to escape a crime
your guiltiness rests upon your tight wall
and you flash your brain forward, fast forward you call

No, no, don't turn it down, no, no, no
Just don't turn it down
I can't turn it off
inside of me.

TERRIBLE TWOS

Baby's got the terrible two's
left with nothing to do
she's so sick with her ears
she's so sick on the floor
the people are walking around her
leaving her to pick up herself
oh yeah she wants attention
you gotta hear my voice
you gotta hear me cry
you gotta try to try it's just terrible two's.

she's sitting up and glancing at you
she's got this tender outrage, she's really alone
Ungodly papa, aren't you?
but she's not a judge
she's only a little bit new
she's not depending on anything that you do
oh yeah, she wants attention
you gotta hear my voice
you've got to hear me cry you've got to try to try
it's just terrible twos

do you remember the days?
it's hidden in your hypnotize
she's just acting her age, she's not a comma
I can't bear to be hurt or be stamped with insults
Hypnotize me now

i'm going to scream!

Enchante

I didn't, I didn't, I didn't know, one thing could lead me to this
I didn't, I didn't, I didn't know, one thing because of a kiss.
Give it to, give it to, give it to me, give me a piece of your heart
give it to, give it to, give it to me, I knew this right from the start.

Enchante, enchante avec amour,
Enchante avec amore,
Enchante, enchante, avec amour
Enchante avec amour

Donne-moi, donne-moi, donne ton coeur
donne t'avec amour
Donne-moi, donne-moi, donne ton coeur
Donne t'avec amour

I didn't, I didn't, I didn't know, one thing could lead me to this
I didn't, I didn't, I didn't know, one thing because of a kiss.
Enchante, enchante avec amour,
enchante avec amour…

enchante, enchante, avec amour enchante avec amour
oh oh
oh, oh, oh, amore
Amore!

Put me in a Trance

I feel the earth shake fast
in the fields, in the snow,
way down below

When we speak, can't speak of voodoo
it's too too blank
I feel your heart so close to mine
blood and fire, panther divine
finger pull out, now push them back in
moon blasts sin

Put me in a trance
Feeling my head spin
I just want to dance
To vivid loud hymns

Expand your love to 200 degrees
Cat comes out from the wall
Athletic brain, I'm down on my knees
sea comes out of the hall'
You've got ruby red lips on the boulevard
I want to paint your face and feel your smile

Put me in a trance
Feeling my head spin
I just want to dance
to vivid loud hymns

Sensing the Sun

Sensing the sun
rain, earth and dirt
of Michigan's story
cornfields so open
strong forests nearby
Sensing the water,
lakes, rivers rebounding
to cleanse our souls and
comfort my own
Sensing remains to envelope love
inside concrete and country
finally the City rises larger
in the dusk of the night
Sense of freedom in Michigan's
summer breezes all my own
love and regret overcomes,
but I'm home.

Shadow

Touch me like the fire
of an ember when its tossed
Our rising, smell the fever
of a trip forever lost
I try so hard to make it work
to realize how much I hurt
Then you come in, you come through
I'll always have you

Worlds overturn, people cry
Lives just burn, I sit and try
to realize all your love is mine
You're like a shadow.

When you're standing close to me
There's nothing could be better
I see you in a fantasy
Reality is fine.
You know the lava burns down deep
you see the constant sadness steep
but after all this misery
you're all that I need.

Once in our great pyramid
the sandy smoke erupts
a tale of two, way down low
we'll feel the shadow.
Worlds overturn, people cry
Lives just burn, I sit and try
to realize all your love is mine
You're like a shadow.

Shiver And Shake

You shiver and you shake
you quiver and you quake
through the rivers and the lakes

taking your mind, it magnifies
the ocean so wide like a long wave strong
and the one that runs is what I become
you got the way to get it right
But you gotta get it right in front of my sight
to move is to make me feel so fine

but you can't stay away when you wanna be mine

driving too fast and driving too far
got to get up and find my star
it's shining in the night and what is it for
to help guide me out there, want so much more
taste on my tongue like cinnamon
tell me that it's going to be okay
hurtling moon through the night
when morning comes, curtain opens tight

grey sky, blue sky, come to me
don't hide a screaming synchronicity
the city so bright burns with all its might
we're going forward like a shining light
cold little shadows on your face
please take me back to a beautiful place

'cause you shiver and you shake
you quiver and you quake.

Circles

Carve my hand, carve my heart
Tattoo daggers now it starts
Crawling around in my mind
Pills shatter through my spine
There's a need to stop and think
I'm memorizing all your tricks
Sanity stops, perhaps it has
Pills do one thing, pills in my hand
Carve a way to get to you
Or else give in to something new
Come on, come on and dance with me
In a holy séance, don't go away

Because I'm fast, but you're faster
Run circles around me
I'm so fast, circle baby
I'm going down

Mr. Love holds us close to the earth
I think it's time to claim my turf
Your voice is smooth like hot buttered rum
Tells me to find the prodigal son
Like a butterfly sent to me
In the middle of the night
I know my path is right
I'm back on track and maybe, baby
I'm a freebird now

Because I'm fast, but you're faster
Run circles around me
I'm so fast, circle baby
I'm going down, down, down
You're so fast, but I'm faster
Run circles around you
I'm so fast, baby, you'll be down

Carve my hand, carve my fist
Baby you got me in a twist
Of lovesick signs, I lose my mind

I take a pill 'cause it feels so fine

Caress my neck like you care
Carve a design in the air
Tell me stories of the man
I'm a freebird now!

Because I'm fast, but you're faster
Run circles around me
I'm so fast, circle baby
I'm going down, down, down

You're so fast, but I'm faster
Run circles around you!! I'm so fast, baby, you'll be down.

Tiara

One girl has spoken
one girl is small
one girl is wading
away from the wall...
she says i'm going down
for the queen on Monday,
i'm the princess i know
for her life i could stay

One girl's the answer
one girl is fall
one girl's just waving
away from the wall
she says i'm going up
going way far away
you will watch me i know
i'm a queen for a day

Tiara tiara tiara
we all fall down
Tiara tiara tiara
wearing a crown

One sister's spoken
one sister's mean
one sister goes for
the way to the Queen
she says i'm going up
going way far away,
I'm the King of the Spades
for her life I will grow

One sister's spoken
one sister's clean
One sister's goes for
the way to the Queen
she says I'm going up,
you will watch me I know
I'm the Queen of the Hearts

for her life I will go

We walk in the garden
Like kings and queens
We feel the presence of everything clean
Tear my hair, tear all that I mean
Lord take me, way far away

Tiara, Tiara, Tiara, we all fall down,
Tiara, Tiara, Tiara, wearing a crown
we all fall down

Look for the light, i will bring it to you
we all fall down wearing a crown
we all fall down wearing a crown.

Honesty

When I woke up
In the morning
Had the TV on without a warning
About those liars and politicians
Who the hell knows what they're dishin'

Let me introduce you
To honesty that you're not used to
Let me entertain you
With Honesty, well it's something new

You're slowing down the future
By thinking in the past
So come on boy let's move into the real world
You come on so strong, your dishonesty's all wrong
It's time to have a real honest heart

With Honesty, it's not a lie
Honesty, it's not a lie
Honesty, it's not a lie
And I told you a long time ago.

Be careful what you're doing
Honesty is revolution
Be careful what you're saying
Honesty is just like praying

You were so relentless
When you lied to me
I could tell you'd someday break my heart
You were just like those talking heads on my TV
I could tell you lied right from the start
Baby, love is all I need
Love is what I breathe
Love is all I need
Love is what?

I relied on honesty
Won't you give me honesty

And tell the truth…about it…

Be careful what you're doing
Honesty is revolution
Be careful what you're saying
Honesty is persecution!

Sing It To Me

One could see it in your face
White dress holding me close
seemed to look so far away
like the Bible was a ghost

if it is I can accept
that myths and lies are not a fact
But I believed I was the best
Sitting in my bright white dress

I said,
Sing it to me, sing it to me, sing it to me, baby
sing it to me, damn my heart

All the children were so cool
They laughed like my aim is true
My life took a little walk
And I could finally talk

Your face gave it all away
Cold shadows only prey
My skin is peeling from the sun
I dyed my hair 'cause now I'm done

Ma said,
Sing it to me, sing it to me, sing it to me, darling
sing it to me, damn my heart

Coal ribbons in my hair
I hate my face up in the crowd
shove rubberbands upon my wrist
To forget what I should have missed

Baby
Sing it to me, sing it to me, sing it to me,
Darling
Sing it to me, sing it to me, sing it to me,
Angel
Sing it to me, sing it to me, sing it to me,

Darling
Sing it to me, sing it to me, sing it to me,

Damn my heart.
Damn my heart, oh, oh—sing.

January Baby

Baby I would love to know all the things in your head
Baby I would love to know all about the dead
Scarlet moon arrest my soul, take me down to my bed
Baby I would love to know all the things in your head

The things I'd learn if I could know
Just where we come from
The winter world is cold and hard
Softer ground lies undone

Baby I would love to know all the things in your head
Baby I would love to know all about the dead
I'm a scarlet moon, arrest my soul and take me down to my bed
I lost control, it's getting old and I forgot what I said

The things I'd learn if I could know
Just where we come from
The winter world is cold and hard
Softer ground lies undone

And baby why'd you love me so
When January was done?
I lost control, it's getting old
But softer ground lies undone
It's softer when I lie undone..

Ocean

Ooh, out the door
Ooh, once more
I walk from the valley
walk from my home
sense some disaster
maybe it's my own...
Ooh, out the door
Ooh, ocean floor

Ooh, out the door
Ooh, once more
I walk from the valley
walk down from the trees
hold down, spin down, spin down, all the way wound, all the way round,
fall down, all the way down, hold on to the trees, to the branches, coming down, spin down, to the sky, all the way down, insane to me now, like outer space

Ooh, out the door
Ooh, ocean floor
Baby, sweet baby,
where did you go?
when you're out there so crazy, where did you go?
I'm feeling so empty,
don't go to sleep
Baby, sweet baby,
my dreams run deep

Ooh out the door
Ooh, ocean floor?

Baby sweet baby, don't go to sleep,
when you're out there so crazy, don't go away,
to the ocean floor
don't close the door
don't close the door
on my heart.

Out in the Streets

We're out in the cold
spraying tastes bold
we don't want to take that
we've got a reaction

They fear us unnerved
But I'm not unfurled
Stoplights squeeze up
Buildings swirl

We're out in the streets
staring down prey
we're out in the streets
In our magic strength days

The earth binds to our spell and we travel well
We wear leather and wool
With our boots jammed full

we've got ecstasy of spirit
now we tumble the light
we're going to thrash all those
who challenge our might

Dark of the soul
now we're ripping out flesh,
they're on a sewer rampage,
concrete could mesh

All right, I sense delirium
ash singes the grave
Doesn't anybody ever go down to the ground?
to rise and save?

No I can't control my heartbeat,
with the opium and starlight
Oh no I can't control my heartbeat
just shut out the lights, they're too bright in the night
You know I feel a hot passion

fanaticism
in rhythm
a prism
we're going to fight all the time
Unite
we're out in the streets, oh yeah!

Blast off Black Magic

Let's start off on a chain reaction
Fortune telling trip under the night
I'm pulling down my shades
I'm chasing out air raids

Let's start off racing hearts as we go
up to a cafe where it's never slow
Jungle lights so hot
where the beat never stops
and a boy chases love all night long

pretty poison to the core
there's no logic anymore
Done some damage to my health
I feel a little bit out of health
Riot's closer all the time, a wild dream in my mind
Now the cave is sinking in and the angel's song begins

Come let me breathe
into love no barricades

reheating all of my chills
with his pace made thrills

frantic panic in my soul
you caught me alone

kamikaze eyes, now I'm not alone

The more you feel
the more you see
the more you're free.

Free

Concrete situation and this place I'm in
Detroit is the story I'm about to begin
Ethnic in fighting and the city is steaming
this is my home and the company I'm keeping

When you're free, you will see
we will lift you up, when you're free
When you're free, you will see
we will lift you up, when you're free

Got the music moving like a ship in the night
cold feelings going without any light
without all the people got to hesitate
pretty hardware all on the gate
Detroit rocks harder, Detroit is so hard
gotta keep on going, pay attention
city's so large
concrete situation and this place I'm in
Detroit is the story I'm about to begin

When you're free, you will see
we will lift you up, when you're free
When you're free, you will see
we will lift you up, when you're free

I can feel the heart of the city
I can know the heart of the city
I can be the heart of the city
And I'm going to fight for my city

Gracious Spoke

Gracious spoke I set my wheels on fire
Set my stage and get beyond a wire
sing to me beyond the wire
Standing soldiers with the fortune song
Love my way and stop to sing along

One fine dance/
 a year of dreams

One fine trance/
 rips at the seams

Steamy skin sweat so sweet

Hot beloved alpha street
Then one fine song

Warmly stands alone
with teardrops revealing on my hand

lasting skies of traveling wings
the bird inside the water sings

 saint
oh
 saint

prayers will bring
city woods
is what remains.
Detroit bells on love parade

Magician of Darkness

The way you feel when you can't see the sun
our paradise is not what you've won
Magician you call yourself
But in the madness of the daylight
Every pore of your skin
fills up with your thoughts
Dignity is not what you've got
You know everybody
but not the right one
to meet this person you can't understand
How can you sleep with your head in the sand
Rolling out of bed, the wood floor soothes (soothes)
Your rude steps and the coffee burns an otherwise frantic mouth
Rush to your car when you should rush to your hands to clasp them
together in prayer
Sin sinner who has not
Man and woman are a repressed lot
You're not alone, but you're all you've got

Not My Design

Pray for rain
For somewhere I can sit
My drink on the wet bar
and just sink
into the abyss
into the atmosphere
to the cold cool glass
where my brain can rest

Holding her hand
when she cries
Telling her it really doesn't matter
Because it's true
To hold her hand
when she dies
and nothing else matters but the truth

Pray for pain
to go away quickly

changes are retained
and the bar is singing slowly

The waitress she pauses
And says it's Not My Design

Stay There

I'm falling in India
I've got a purple stained revolver
and a little rain was falling
the smell was getting stronger
shaking like a leaf
don't know what to do
all these laws imposed,
who are you?
So we ran into an icestorm
and we wondered, why the crashing?

You never knew
I wanted you
Lies you read about
make me want to

shout stay there.

He's covered in chords
He's like a kamikaze flier
you know he wants to save the day
but he's got dripping eyeliner

Where'd he go?

You never knew
I wanted you
Lies you read about
make me want to

SHOUT Marching, Marching,
Who are you?
Marching, Marching,
Don't know what to do
Marching, Marching
Who are you?
Marching, marching
well you think you're cool, but you're not.

Transcendence Captured from a Distance

Captured from a distance
you take my picture
I keep the lens
capture my resistance
it's so easy for you
to say what to send
rapture, my existence when I look in your eyes
it's heaven's gain
dashing your insistence
that my face is near yours in the wind

Everything I ever wanted it's right here
everything I ever smoked for
purple haze to die for
everything you want to capture
it's right here
the way that I love you
it's right here
capture every moment over here

longing, that's what I hope for
to want and hope for
love on my lips
desire, it's a strong word
you know when I speak
do it for you
absolutely, pure and simple
like my blouse next to my skin
as I lay heavy, in transudation
translucent fingers tough my own
under within

Everything I ever wanted
it's right here
everything I ever pined for, got high for
it's right here
the way that I love you
it's right here
capture every moment
over here

Something Special

woke up and I realized time was gone
the bombs had quieted to a new dawn
with my favorite little sweater
wrapped around a little better
I could see light outside the wall
We've been sitting here for way too long
I've starting wondering why we must be strong
what if I just ran out screaming, loving life that's too revealing…

why can't I have something special
I wake up and smile
the love I have is strong and restful
I feel like a spy

the soldiers' voices echo near and far
they are out there in the killing jar
I've met a boy, it's something different
all these feelings now I'm in it
who can I talk to if not you?

the moon is getting strong it lights my face
we are moving to a better place
there is a free world it's out there
somewhere far where I can dance

Why can't I have something special
to wake up and smile
the love I have is strong and restful
I feel like a spy

When you very small, I knew you'd do what I say
because you love because you love me because you love me like you do

Cold Summer June

Tudor out girl
stop the whirl
liars everywhere
when people stop and blurt it out
Find love in the air
Please explain, don't hold me up
I really got to know
you're a jerk
but I love you
Is that makes me more alert, mercurial?

Watery eyes
Watery sighs, thicken out the room
smoke is getting in our eyes
sky so green with doom
The old man and The Sea once more
come crawling in the morning light
Thunderstorm comes crashing
waves seem ever lasting
Wish I had your passion
Yet I'm frozen although it's June
in the gloom
all too soon

Freighters coming in down the lake
Honest in their voyage
Camouflaged
like your face, and seek descending on their voyage
arrival time
you're sick of signs, point to façade
I know you are creepy and nothing like a God
That's OK, it's supposed to be
summer in this room
The waves are hitting icebergs
we're frozen though it's JUNE

Out Of Tune

Out of tune in your room
Can't hear the sneeze, feel a breeze
it's time you do, can you be bold
wasn't meant for development, then pitch a tent he said
Don't lie to me
Oh Goddess soul
be well, be real and benevolent
and not superficial, prevalent

I remember April 5, 1995.

We played at the Ark with Patti Smith. It was coming out to a new adventure with praise, hours in the studio and onstage, hours of music, hours of songs and books, hours of keyboards and hours of travel about to begin again.

But then again, I spent hours in the air going to Japan way back in the 1980's, hours of hours of hours and working and working and working and college and college and stages and studios back to stages and rehearsals, practice makes perfect and practice and practice...

Often onstage, during an emotional part of a song, I get in a moment and have to visit it later, hours after spending time on this subconscious kind of thinking and then analyzing. This is an opening—not Opening Day (Go Tigers!)—but a kind of obsessive sparring. Maybe that's all it is. A beginning is again over and over and a mind needs to stop and let it go. But a new beginning is like the new promise and new recollections to grasp.

In *Bladerunner*, Roy says, "All these memories will be lost...in time..." and "I have seen things no one has seen..ships on fire on Orion, all these things... lost in time." In Mary Shelley's *Frankenstein*, the pain of death touches us so harshly we wish to bring back and hold onto those we love and ensure "this will not happen again!"

In a sense, maybe separation and moving, traveling and a new song, new chapter, new job is a similar emotion. It's either you can't wait to do it. Or you dread it. What's it going to be? Scary experiences or exciting new adventures? So does this breed newness ? Or does change become a death of independence because you're no longer carefree? Well, it's a new chapter or a new window. A big huge change brings anxiety, no matter how positive or negative.

Considering birth or creating new—Victor Frankenstein's monster with feelings and emotion was only responding to environment and abandonment. So if we abandon one dream for another, are we shutting down and hurting what could have been? Or are we substituting one birth long ago for one that is destined to be a repeat of our initial proposal?

I'm getting ahead of myself. But consider that a new album could be new for how long? It then is "old' again and fades away, as everything does.

So how can we call something new when time goes so fast that nothing is new anymore?

Finally, can we ever think again about communally instead of individually and give birth to helping each other? Is there a way to stop being so competitive and instead, caring?

Of course, so much depends on a red wheelbarrow as William Carlos Williams said. And that red wheelbarrow is a choice. So do we have a real choice or is it Destiny planned?

Italy

Cast in a film
My part is of villain
Or saber toothed Tiger
one just a liar

Holds onto sane
girl
do I need you now
girl
do I wish you were here
with me now, You, you save me from myself.
I love you so much
I wish you were ice with me, holding me.

Apres midi 7

J'ai faim pour amour et je triste et excite.

Could it be, what I want is me?
Me to love, me to see?
Eye to eye with me.
Lord above, Lord hear my prayer.
Let me love the way I care.
Give me, my daily light to shine
My heart so open all the time.

Could it be? I should need a special love I thought I had?
Is it me that I need? Can I really love me?

One More Round (into the night)

One alone, cast a spell
over her heart
she was nothing, she was something
right from the start

sorry here and sorry there
I'm sorry alone
to bring you sad
to make you mad
God on the phone

Snow in the streetlights
all coming down
Snow in the starlight
all over town

Love is watching
in the zone
love is twilight underneath your hidden
stories
and your glowing
just like
last night

Sorry here and sorry there
will not hurt you now
You're together in your heart
and You're not alone

Snow in the streetlights
 it's coming down
Snow in the starlight
of freedom and one more ROUND

Romantic River of Weird Times

No news is impossible
no matter how you try
you change with everything
to fit in
to
try
to win

something

to change
then
say

what?

then you go back again
because what
it is
is not
always impossible
so to be

King of the Road

Red fire truck
engine
screaming
on some wave in St Petersburg
melting time on the beach
Dali within reach
of
another symptom
of distress

sirens and horns
on the lawn
bones holding
intact
tiny car
spinning in space
tempo of music
tempo of face
tempo hurting
me as I hold on tight

a cowgirl
who has a crush
on steel metal

she goes and holds
the steering wheel
in the stream of a red dress
firing up the fire truck
swerving lanes
kissing the center
head of the road
I'm going to duck and run

no way, the sun
is not going to kill me
here
yet.

Sun Blues

the sun is coming out
it is painful
when you're feeling this way
I can't teach anyone anything
I can only show them
it's not that I matter
but they matter
and I stare at the shredded paper
and piles of memories
each becoming sad

April is the Cruelest Month

She played out her nights in frozen skies
darkness of winter so cold
She's spending her life in a room like a stone
Just let it go and let your heart be
Loosen the tight rope around sensitivity

Sing it to me, sing it again
Because starting over feels like a friend
Sing it to me with love and no fear
April so cold it arouses a tear

This month is a long one, it seems so bewildered
The ground is so cold, it feels so deliberate
And April, it's April, and cruel that it is
Wrap around fingers a feeling of misery.

Giftwrapped in Cool

It starts when you're always angry
Starts so slow it's not there
But you can see it coming
But you don't know from where

You're going to run for a couple of hours
throw yourself at the mirror
Dim yourself in a spotlight
Like nobody will care

'Cause everybody tells you what to do
everybody tells you what to do
Know so much but you can't get through
Don't forget you're giftwrapped in cool

Outside there is resentment
inside me is a choir
you stand outside on the sidewalk
looking love in the eye

You're going to run for a couple of hours
Sweat 'till you feel ill
Hold yourself in a spotlight
like nobody will care

'Cause everybody tells you what to do
everybody tells you what to do
Know so much but you can't get through
Don't forget you're giftwrapped in cool

It starts when you're always angry
Starts so slow it's not there
But you can see it coming
But you don't know from where

You're going to run for a couple of hours
throw yourself at the mirror
Dim yourself in a spotlight
love without any fear!

'Cause everybody tells you what to do
everybody tells you what to do
Know so much but you can't get through
Don't forget you're giftwrapped in cool

Acknowledgments

This book would not be possible without my family and the artists, musicians, friends and memories of growing up and living in Detroit, but also the beauty of Michigan, the underdog struggle and streets, and the big, beautiful world.

To so many muses: Including so many of my musician heroes, artist and writer heroes, far and way too many to name, but this is a start: especially Bob Marley, Patti Smith, David Bowie, Lou Reed, Iggy and The Stooges/Iggy Pop, The Ramones, Sparks, Nina Simone, Grace Jones, Bela Bartok, James Brown, Yoko Ono, Fred "Sonic" Smith, Tower of Power, Blondie, Suzi Quatro, Marvin Gaye, The Runaways, Jobim and Gilberto, Motown, Patsy Cline, Little Richard, Roxy Music, The Monkees, Prince, Johnny Cash, Sly and The Family Stone, The Jacksons, Carole King, Joni Mitchell, Talking Heads, The Clash, Television, Dead Kennedys, Stevie Wonder, The Stones, The Temptations, Satie, Chopin and Beethoven, Jimi Hendrix, Bjork, The Doors, John Lee Hooker, The Slits, PJ Harvey, The Beatles, Anne Frank, Shakespeare, Queen, MC5, Diane Di Prima, The Beat Poets, Emily Dickinson, Frida Kahlo, Picasso, Dali, Jackson Pollock, Charles Bukowski, French cinema, Marge Piercy, Maya Angelou, Hemingway, Salinger, Lorraine Hansberry, *The Wizard of Oz, To Sir With Love, Apocalypse Now, The Sound of Music* and way too many more to list. Also to the inspiration of cabaret, blues and jazz, bossa nova, gypsy czardas, polkas and my surfy-sounding Farfisa organ.

To my family: My late Mom and Dad, who encouraged me to play music, perform, write and create, I am so grateful. To my sister, Patti, and our antics growing up, and nieces Tiffany, Maria and Alayna, nephew Travis, also stepdaughter Nicole and stepson Nika, and my cousins, aunts, uncles, grandparents, and brother-in-law Craig. And to my stepmom Phyllis and her daughter Linda. xo. Special thank you to Freddie Brooks, who never doubted I could write and make music.

To my friends who loved me no matter what: Rest in peace to Cooper, Brim, Lyn, Butch, Kenny, Buster, Kerry, Eddie and many more.

And to my co-conspirator, guitarist and singer/songwriter in his own right: My dear husband and guitarist, the talented Scott Dailey, to whom I am so eternally grateful. I love you so much.

To my music family: The great Detroit musicians I have worked with, from my current band Carolyn Striho Group to Detroit Energy Asylum to Rough Cut and way back to The Cubes (and Prong). You have graced my and our albums, CDs, vinyl, and cassettes with your inspiring, beautiful and intriguing musicianship. I love you.

To the students and creators of the future: Unite, create, don't compete and remember, People Have The Power.

And thanks for you, Heather Buchanan and Aquarius Press.

About the Author

Carolyn mesmerizes audiences with her strong vocals, fiery keyboard and guitar, energetic performances, heartfelt and poetic melodies, spontaneous improvisation, torch songs and dance beats, but also with a gypsy flourish of modern music. Carolyn's most recent album, *Afterthought,* was on the GRAMMY® Awards 2018 First Ballot for Best Rock Album of the Year. Carolyn has won 11 Detroit Music Awards and a Billboard Magazine Award for her songwriting, albums, musicianship and live performances. Carolyn also has toured overseas six times in Europe, and also had a two-month tour of Japan. She's played many national and international festivals including Lollapalooza, Rome Italy's Donne In Musica, London U.K. Meltdown, and many more. Carolyn's musical resume is quite extensive, with highlights including opening for Steve Earle in England, and performing in Detroit, Toronto, Chicago, Frascati, Fiuggi and Rome, Italy and in London and Isle of Wight, U.K. Carolyn's also performed with Patti Smith on two tours, and with her band, Detroit Energy Asylum, which included many members of Was (Not Was). With a strong catalog of music, she is working on a new album for 2020 and a new U.K. tour.

Carolyn is a Wayne State University Graduate (B.A., M.S., Ed.S.) and also a high school English teacher in Special Education in Metro Detroit. She has more memories of her DJ life on the radio (NPR/WDET-FM) and working in a law firm, and now lives in the Detroit area with her husband, Scott Dailey, and kitty.

www.carolynstriho.com

www.ingramcontent.com/pod-product-compliance
Lightning Source LLC
Chambersburg PA
CBHW060341080526
44584CB00013B/865